## SPORTS ALL-STARS

# ANTONIO BROWN

Jon M. Fishman

Lerner Publications ◆ Minneapolis

Lerner Publications Company
A division of Lerner Publishing Group, Inc.
241 First Avenue North
Minneapolis, MN 55401 USA

For reading levels and more information, look up this title at www.lernerbooks.com.

**Library of Congress Cataloging-in-Publication Data**

Names: Fishman, Jon M., author.
Title: Antonio Brown / Jon M. Fishman.
Description: Minneapolis, MN : Lerner Publications Company, [2019] | Series: Sports all-stars | Includes bibliographical references and index. | Audience: Age 7–11. | Audience: Grade 4 to 6.
Identifiers: LCCN 2017057017 (print) | LCCN 2017058802 (ebook) | ISBN 9781541524637 (eb pdf) | ISBN 9781541524552 (lb : alk. paper) | ISBN 9781541528017 (pb : alk. paper)
Subjects: LCSH: Brown, Antonio, 1988—Juvenile literature. | Football players—United States—Biography—Juvenile literature.
Classification: LCC GV939.B733 (ebook) | LCC GV939.B733 F57 2019 (print) | DDC 796.332092 [B]—dc23

LC record available at https://lccn.loc.gov/2017057017

Manufactured in the United States of America
1 - 44531 - 34781 - 4/19/2018

# CONTENTS

# LEGEND IN THE MAKING

Antonio Brown runs in for a touchdown on October 15, 2017.

**Antonio Brown was on fire.** The Pittsburgh Steelers **wide receiver** leaped. He snatched the ball out of the air for a 17-yard gain. The play gave Brown six catches and almost 100 receiving yards for the game. But he was just getting started.

Brown and his teammates were playing against the Kansas City Chiefs on October 15, 2017. The Steelers were ahead late in the fourth quarter, 12–10, but they wanted to score again to secure the win.

With less than six minutes remaining in the game, Brown caught a pass for 10 yards.

Two plays later, Pittsburgh quarterback Ben Roethlisberger stepped forward. He launched the ball down the field—right to a Kansas City defender. But the defender couldn't hold onto the ball. It bounced, flipped, and landed in Brown's hands.

Brown catches the ball after it bounced away from a Chiefs player.

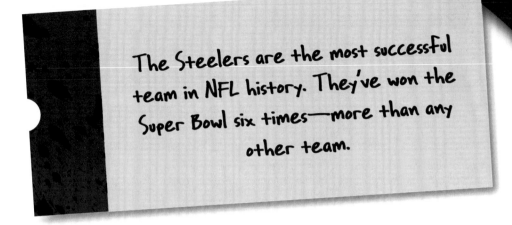

The Steelers are the most successful team in NFL history. They've won the Super Bowl six times—more than any other team.

Pittsburgh's superstar wide receiver sprinted 51 yards down the field with the ball tucked in his left arm. No one could catch him. He scored a touchdown to extend Pittsburgh's lead. They won the game, 19–13.

Brown had 155 receiving yards in the game. His long touchdown was the 52nd of his career. That gave him one more touchdown than Pittsburgh legend Lynn Swann and the third most in Steelers history. Fans expect Brown will set more records in coming years as he becomes a football legend of his own.

Brown plays in a college football game in 2009.

**On July 10, 1988, Antonio Brown was born in Miami, Florida.** His parents, Eddie and Adrianne, were high school students. About a year later, Eddie went to play college football in Louisiana. Adrianne stayed in Miami to care for

Although they never played together, Antonio and Indianapolis Colts wide receiver T. Y. Hilton both grew up in Miami, Florida.

Antonio and his younger brother, Desmond. Later, Antonio's parents broke up.

Antonio loved playing football. Most kids start out playing touch football or flag football. Yet Antonio began playing tackle football when he was just six years old. One of his youth coaches remembers Antonio's love for the sport: "[Antonio would] say, 'Coach, I can play quarterback too! I was wide open, Coach!'"

Brown runs down the field in a college game against the Ohio Bobcats in 2009.

Antonio proved that he could play quarterback at Norland High School in Miami. He was smaller than many high school quarterbacks, but he was confident and fast. Then trouble at home distracted him from schoolwork and football. Antonio left home at the age of 16 to care for himself.

Suddenly, surviving on the streets of Miami became Antonio's focus. He slept on friends' couches. Sometimes, he slept in a friend's car. Through it all, he excelled on the football field. Colleges with big-time football teams **recruited** him. But it's hard to do well in school when you don't have a place to do homework. Antonio's grades weren't good enough for many schools.

Brown was determined to play college football. In 2006, he attended North Carolina Tech. He played quarterback for the **prep school** and improved his grades. The next year, he got a shot to play at Central Michigan University (CMU).

The coaches at CMU noticed that Brown wasn't as tall as most college quarterbacks. Instead, they wanted him to play wide receiver. His speed and **agility** made him a good fit for the position.

Brown learned his new position quickly. He caught about 100 passes in each of his three seasons at CMU. It was enough to draw the attention of NFL **scouts**. In 2010, the Steelers chose him with the 195th pick in the **NFL Draft**.

Brown shows off his skills during a Pittsburgh Steelers practice in 2010.

The Pittsburgh Steelers practice together before the season starts.

**On game days, NFL players don't hold anything back.** They spend the rest of the week working out and practicing for games. During the season, players usually get just one day each

Brown stretches his legs before a game in 2016.

week to rest and relax. Brown works out as if the season lasts all year. "My goal in the **off-season** is to be as disciplined as during the season," he says.

Brown focuses many of his workouts on his legs. Strong legs help him run past defenders and soar to catch footballs. Sometimes he does exercises such as **squats** with heavy weights. Other times he may jump onto a bench from side to side without using weights.

He also spends plenty of time running, both long distances and **sprints**.

Special gear helps Brown stay ready for game action. He may run with a parachute trailing him to make each step more difficult. He uses heavy vests to weigh him down. Sometimes he wears a training mask when he runs that reduces the amount of air he can breathe. It makes his body work harder for every breath.

Brown warms up with a training mask before a game in 2017.

Brown does a variety of exercises using resistance bands. They look like big rubber bands. He sometimes wraps them around his legs or body when he works out. The bands provide resistance similar to heavy weights and help Brown become more **flexible**. Athletes are also less likely to get injured using resistance bands.

Brown loves to swim too. A pool workout gets his heart beating quickly when he needs a break from heavy weights and intense runs. He says he sometimes holds his breath for up to 12 **laps** to strengthen his lungs!

A healthful diet fuels Brown's workouts. He eats plenty of nutritious foods such as egg whites, chicken, and oatmeal. A personal chef prepares his meals and makes sure the superstar receiver stays on track with his diet. Of course, sometimes Brown strays from the plan. Steak, tacos, and Starburst candy are some of his favorite treats.

People must get enough sleep to perform their best. Brown sticks to a strict sleep schedule during the season. "But in the off-season, I only get four or five hours—it's hard to sleep when you're having a lot of fun," Brown says.

# DANCING LIKE A STAR

Brown dances after scoring a touchdown in a 2014 game against the Cincinnati Bengals.

**"Chest up.** Eyes Up. Prayed Up." Brown often repeats these words to himself. "I've been using that since I was a kid," he says. He thinks about the words when he wants to feel more confident.

Brown and Dwayne Johnson (*above*) encourage each other during their workouts together.

Reminding himself to stay strong and confident has helped Brown reach the top of the sports world. It has also helped him shine off the field. You've probably seen him in a TV commercial. He's appeared on lots of TV shows too, including *MVP* and *Shark Tank*. He's even worked with famous actors such as Dwayne "the Rock" Johnson.

Brown poses with his Dancing with the Stars partner, Sharna Burgess.

Brown enjoys dancing on and off the field!

One of Brown's most popular TV appearances came in 2016. He joined *Dancing with the Stars* and wowed fans with his smooth moves on the dance floor. Brown and partner Sharna Burgess made it all the way to the show's **semifinal** round.

Pittsburgh fans weren't surprised by his dancing ability. Brown has been dancing after scoring touchdowns since he joined the NFL. He spins and twists. He shakes his hips and swings his arms. He's always thinking about new ways to have a good time on the field.

# Riding in Style

When Brown joined the **NFL** in 2010, he didn't have much money. He saved most of what he earned during his first two seasons. Then, in 2012, Pittsburgh agreed to pay him almost $42 million over the next five years. To celebrate, he bought a car: a brand-new Rolls-Royce.

In 2017, Brown and the Steelers agreed to an even bigger deal. The four-year, $68 million agreement made him the best-paid wide receiver in football. Brown celebrated with another Rolls-Royce. Brown hired a **chauffeur** to drive him to practice in the car.

Brown rolled up to Steelers practice in a classic Rolls-Royce like this one.

Another fun part of being a superstar athlete is having your own trading cards. Brown was thrilled the first time he saw his face on a card. He still keeps some of his first NFL cards in his locker. As a kid, he collected NFL player cards as well as Pokémon trading cards.

Brown spends a lot of time helping people in his community. In December 2016, he gave $100,000 to Children's Hospital of Pittsburgh. His family inspired him to bring joy to children in need. He helped 800 kids in the Pittsburgh area get new backpacks in 2017. He even holds a celebrity softball tournament that helps youth groups.

# SUPER BOWL GOAL

Brown gets around a Baltimore Ravens player in a 2010 game.

**Many football stars play the same position throughout their careers.** By the time they reach the NFL, a player may have 10 years or more of experience. But Brown had been playing wide receiver for a only few years when he joined

Brown catches a pass during a preseason game in 2010.

the NFL. Suddenly, he had to prove himself against the world's toughest players.

Brown had to fight for his chance to play during his first season in 2010. The Steelers had four receivers with more experience, and Brown spent a lot of time on the bench. He played in just nine of the team's 16 regular-season games. But when he got onto the field,

Brown runs with the ball during the 2012 Pro Bowl.

he made sure his coaches noticed him. Brown's big plays helped the Steelers reach the Super Bowl. Pittsburgh lost to the Green Bay Packers, 31–25.

The Steelers quickly realized that Brown could be a great player. By 2011, he was a major part of Pittsburgh's plan for every game. He caught a 79-yard pass that was the longest touchdown catch of his NFL career. Brown made the **Pro Bowl** team for the first time.

Brown watches for defenders as he races down the field.

In 2014, Brown led all NFL players with 1,698 receiving yards. He finished second in yards in two other seasons. In fewer than eight full NFL seasons, Brown has totaled almost 10,000 receiving yards. With such incredible numbers, he is beginning to be compared to the greatest pass catchers of all time. Jerry Rice holds almost all the league's receiving records. Could Brown catch Rice and become the best receiver ever?

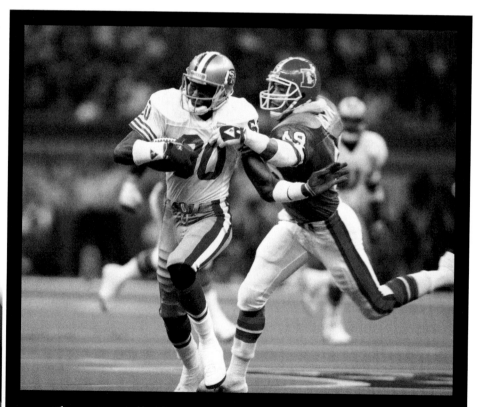

Jerry Rice (left) is considered to be the best wide receiver in NFL history.

Brown makes an impressive catch in a game in 2014.

For all that he's already done, Brown still has a long way to go before he catches up to Rice and other NFL legends. Brown's talent is incredible. But he knows that it takes more than talent to become a football legend. "I've proved I can do all those things," he said. "The goal left for me is to win the Super Bowl."

# All-Star Stats

The Pittsburgh Steelers are one of the NFL's oldest teams. They started out in 1933 as the Pittsburgh Pirates. The name changed to the Steelers in 1940. The team has had plenty of fantastic players in their long history. Brown has shown that he may be the best yet. Here's where he ranks on the team's all-time receiving yards list:

| Player | Receiving Yards |
| --- | --- |
| Hines Ward | 12,083 |
| Antonio Brown | 9,212 |
| John Stallworth | 8,723 |
| Heath Miller | 6,569 |
| Louis Lipps | 6,018 |
| Lynn Swann | 5,462 |
| Elbie Nickel | 5,131 |
| Buddy Dial | 4,723 |
| Plaxico Burress | 4,206 |
| Mike Wallace | 4,042 |

# Source Notes

9    Mina Kimes, "After a Decade Apart, Antonio Brown and T.Y. Hilton Share an Unlikely Bond," *ESPN*, November 24, 2015, http://www.espn.com/nfl/story/_/id/14179705/antonio-brown -ty-hilton-unlikely-bond.

13   "NFL Up! with Antonio Brown," video, *NFL Up!*, accessed November 4, 2017, http://up.nfl.com/workout/antonio-brown -top-tier-speed/70.

15   Morty Ain, "Brown: 'Being Passed Up Because of My Size Made Me Hungry,'" *ESPN*, July 5, 2016, http://www.espn .com/nfl/story/_/page/bodyantoniobrown/pittsburgh-steelers -wide-receiver-antonio-brown-talks-starbursts-mango-season -body-issue-2016.

16   Dan Gigler, "Steelers WR Brown Overcomes Mean Streets of Miami," *Pittsburgh Post-Gazette*, December 24, 2011, http://www.post-gazette.com/sports/steelers/2011/12/24 /Steelers-WR-Brown-overcomes-mean-streets-of-Miami /stories/201112240151.

27   Jeremy Fowler, "Antonio Brown Has Stats; Wants Super Bowl to Define Legacy," *ESPN*, January 4, 2017, http://www.espn .com/blog/pittsburgh-steelers/post/_/id/22165/antonio-brown -comes-to-grips-with-legacy-its-not-all-about-stats.

**agility:** ability to move quickly and smoothly

**chauffeur:** a person who is paid to drive a car

**flexible:** able to bend easily

**laps:** trips around a pool

**NFL Draft:** an event in which NFL teams take turns choosing new players

**off-season:** the part of the year when a sports league is not playing

**prep school:** a school that prepares students for college

**Pro Bowl:** a game held each year to honor that season's best NFL players

**recruited:** selected to add a player to a team

**scouts:** people who judge the skills of athletes

**semifinal:** the next to last round in a tournament

**sprints:** short runs done as fast as possible

**squats:** an exercise that involves low crouches to strengthen the legs

**wide receiver:** a player whose main job is to catch passes

Monnig, Alex. *Antonio Brown: Football Star*. Mendota Heights, MN: North Star Editions, 2018.

Morey, Allan. *The Pittsburgh Steelers Story*. Minneapolis: Bellwether Media, 2017.

NFL Rush
http://www.nflrush.com

Pittsburgh Steelers
http://www.steelers.com

Savage, Jeff. *Football Super Stats*. Minneapolis: Lerner Publications, 2018.

*Sports Illustrated Kids*
https://www.sikids.com

# Index

# Photo Acknowledgments

Image credits: iStock.com/63151 (gold and silver stars); Rob Carr/Getty Images, p. 2; Peter Aiken/Getty Images, pp. 4–5, 6; Mark Cunningham/Getty Images, pp. 8, 10; cate_89/Shutterstock.com, p. 9; Gregory Shamus/Getty Images, p. 11; Mark Alberti/ Icon Sportswire/Getty Images, p. 12; George Gojkovich/Getty Images, pp. 13, 19; Zach Bolinger/Icon Sportswire/Getty Images, p. 14; Justin Berl/Icon Sportswire/Getty Images, p. 16; VCG/Getty Images, p. 17; Bruce Glikas/FilmMagic/Getty Images, p. 18; Leena Robinson/Shutterstock.com, p. 20; Doug Kapustin/MCT/Getty Images, p. 22; Jared Wickerham/Getty Images, p. 23; Kent Nishimura/Getty Images, p. 24; Andy Lyons/Getty Images, p. 25; Rich Pilling/Sporting News/Getty Images, p. 26; Justin K. Aller/Getty Images, p. 27.

Cover: Rob Carr/Getty Images; iStock.com/neyro2008.